P9-CCQ-804

THE PORTABLE 7 HABITS™

Abundance

Fulfilling Your Potential for Success

Other Portable 7 Habits Books
Choice: Choosing the Proactive Life You Want to Live
Vision: Defining Your Destiny in Life
Purpose: Focusing on What Matters Most
Trust: Sharing Ideas, Insights, and Understanding
Synergy: Connecting to the Power of Cooperation
Renewal: Nourishing Body, Mind, Heart, and Soul

Other Books from Franklin Covey
The 7 Habits of Highly Effective People
The 7 Habits of Highly Effective Families
The 7 Habits of Highly Effective Teens
The 7 Habits of Highly Effective Teens Journal
Daily Reflections for Highly Effective Teens
Daily Reflections for Highly Effective People
Living the 7 Habits

Loving Reminders for Kids
Loving Reminders for Couples
Loving Reminders for Families
Loving Reminders Teen to Teen
Loving Reminders to Make Kids Laugh
Quotes and Quips

Franklin Covey
2200 West Parkway Boulevard
Salt Lake City, Utah 84119-2099

©2000 by Franklin Covey Co. 9910031 All rights reserved, including the right of reproduction
in whole or in part in any form. This book is the proprietary work of Franklin Covey Co. Many terms in this
book, including the title, are trademarks of Franklin Covey Co. Any unauthorized use of this copyrighted
material or use of any of these terms in relation to goods and/or services (including
seminars, workshops, training programs, classes, etc.) is prohibited without the express written
permission of the owner.

Concept: Cheryl Kerzner
Design: Jenny Peterson
Illustration: Tammy Smith
Written and compiled by Debra Harris
Contributors: John Crowley, Ann Hobson, Sunny Larson, Shelley Orgill

Manufactured in United States of America

ISBN 1-929494-12-2

CONTENTS

Our generosity towards others is key to our positive experience of the world. There's enough room for everyone to be beautiful. There's enough room for everyone to be successful. There's enough room for everyone to be rich. It is only our thinking that blocks that possibility from happening.

——MARIANNE WILLIAMSON

INTRODUCTION

To live a rich life, it's imperative to believe in your ability to prosper—that you are deserving. Once understood and embraced, an abundance mentality allows you to see your life and your relationships from a new perspective. It's about sharing the wealth and focusing on the universal truth that there is truly enough in this world for everyone.

In *Abundance: Fulfilling Your Potential for Success*, we've simplified the powerful principles behind *The 7 Habits of Highly Effective People* by Stephen R. Covey to help you discover the easiest and most fulfilling ways to live an abundant lifestyle.

There are no roadmaps to follow. No instructions. No how-tos. And no formulas for success. Instead you'll find a collection of contemporary quotes, thought-provoking questions, provocative messages, and practical wisdom in an easy-to-read format.

As you turn these pages, take the words of advice to heart, mind, body, and soul. Think about what you read. Ponder how and what it would take to interact more successfully in your everyday life. Let the wisdom inspire you to become more generous with yourself and others in order to reap the benefits. Which means getting rid of "all about me" thinking and developing an everyone-can-win mind-set.

In essence, make it a habit to think Win-Win.

HABIT 4: THINK WIN-WIN®

Acquire an everyone-can-win attitude.

INTERACTION

The person who is truly effective has the humility and reverence to recognize his own perceptual limitations and to appreciate the rich resources available through interaction with the hearts and minds of other human beings.

——STEPHEN R. COVEY, *The 7 Habits of Highly Effective People*

I am he as you are we and **we are all together.**

—JOHN LENNON AND PAUL McCARTNEY

4

You can't be truly interdependent until you've built a strong foundation of

INDEPENDENCE FIRST.

Kindness

is more important than wisdom,
and the recognition of this is the
beginning of wisdom.

—THEODORE ISAAC RUBIN

The more you try to be interested in other people, the more you find out about yourself.

—THEA ASTLEY

Is It My Imagination, or Is This the Age of the Control Freak?

I'm standing in front of the triceps machine at the gym. I've just set the weights, and I'm about to begin my exercise when a lightly muscled bully in turquoise spandex interrupts her chest presses to bark at me, "I'm using that," she growls as she leaps up from her slant board, darts over to the triceps machine and resets the weights. I'm tempted to point out, while she may have been planning to use the machine, she was, in fact, on the opposite side of the room. And that her muscles won't atrophy if she waits for me to finish. Instead, I work on my biceps. Life's too short to fight over a Nautilus machine. Of course, I'm not a control freak. Control freaks will fight over anything: a parking place, the room temperature, the last pair of marked-down Maude Frizon pumps, even whether you should barbecue with the top on or off the Weber kettle. Nothing is too insignificant. Everything has to be just so.

—MARGO KAUFMAN

Go ahead.

Make someone else's day.

Negotiating Win-Win outcomes may feel challenging for some because most people enjoy being right, and they prefer to win rather than conceding to their partner's point of view. For many, compromise means to be weaker or inferior to your opponent. It means to give up what you want and settle for something that is less than you originally desired. However, in a Win-Win outcome, **there is no concession,** as both people walk away from the negotiation feeling gratified that both of them got what they wanted.

—CHÉRIE CARTER-SCOTT

*S*ee more in someone else than they are showing you.

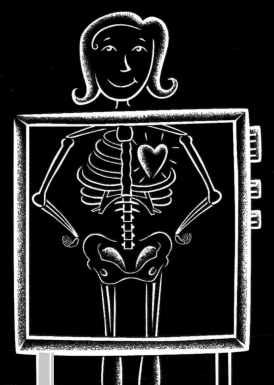

How to Negotiate a Win-Win

> **Disclose what you need and want right up front.** Bring all your intentions to the party.

> **Figure out what you both want out of the situation.** Develop a purpose statement that is absolutely true for both people. Agree on the statement and refer to it as a tool to keep negotiations on track.

> **Develop a plan of who wants what and why.** Discuss in general terms how to make it happen. Write down ideas on how to reach the desired goal that is a win for both of you.

> **Keep working through options and alternatives until you get closer to an agreement.** Be prepared to hammer out any difficult steps with courtesy, respect, and appreciation for the other point of view. Once the other person sees that you really want to resolve the issue with a win for both of you, it will be easier to come to an agreement.

> **Reach a mutual agreement.** Don't forget to congratulate yourselves for being mature enough to make decisions that benefit everyone concerned.

> **If you can't find a solution that benefits all concerned, agree to a no-deal solution.** It's better not to deal than to live with a decision that isn't right.

Real friends

are those who when you've made an absolute fool of yourself, don't feel that you've done a permanent job.

Can you stop viewing the world through I-glasses?

CHARACTER

The real key to your influence with me is your example...the kind of person you truly are—not what others say you are or what you may want me to think you are...Your character is constantly radiating, communicating. From it, I come to instinctively trust or distrust you and your efforts with me.

—STEPHEN R. COVEY, *The 7 Habits of Highly Effective People*

CHARACTER

is the architecture of the being.

—LOUISE NEVELSON

Often people attempt to live their lives backwards; they try to have more things, or more money, in order to do more of what they want, so they will be happier. The way it actually works is the reverse. You must first be who you really are, then do what you need to do, in order to

have what you want.

—MARGARET YOUNG

Experiences That Will
STRENGTHEN
Your Character

• Getting audited.

• Getting fired.

• Waitressing.

• Vacationing with your three best friends.

—LESLEY DORMEN

A person's **true character** is revealed by what he does when no one else is watching.

Your true religion is the

life you live,

not the creed you profess.

—UNKNOWN

Integrity is never painless.

—M. SCOTT PECK

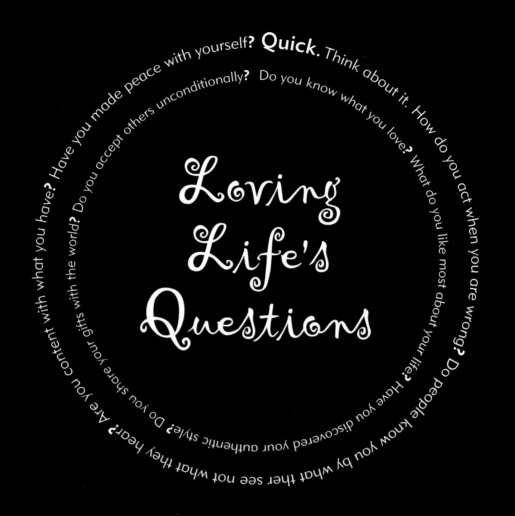

Have you made peace with yourself? **Quick.** Think about it. How do you act when you are wrong? Do people know you by what they see not what they hear? Do you share your gifts with the world? Do you accept others unconditionally? Do you know what you love? What do you like most about your life? Have you discovered your authentic style? Are you content with what you have?

Loving Life's Questions

PERFECTIONISM

is self-abuse of the highest order.

—ANNE WILSON SCHAEF

Do you feel threatened when a friend or coworker succeeds? Remember this:

there's enough success
for everyone.

Recite it over and over to yourself the next time you get hit with yet another whiney "Why not me?" moment.

Take care of your character
and your reputation will take care of itself.

To live each day as though one's last, never flustered, never apathetic, never attitudinizing—here is the perfection of character.

—MARCUS AURELIUS

GROWTH

Taking initiative does not mean being pushy, obnoxious, or aggressive. It does mean recognizing your responsibility to make things happen.

——STEPHEN R. COVEY, *The 7 Habits of Highly Effective People*

EXPERIENCE

is how life catches up with us and teaches us to love and forgive each other.

—LOUISE NEVELSON

𝒯here is so much in the world for us all if we only have the eyes to see it, and the heart to love it, and the hand to gather it to ourselves.

—LUCY MAUD MONTGOMERY

BIG PEOPLE

are those who make us feel bigger

when we're around them.

Who am I to think I'm so special
that I'm not allowed to make mistakes?

When did I come up with that?

I'm fully and totally culpable for all of my
errors, but...I am also fully responsible
for all the wonderful successes of my life.
And that's a huge thing.

—JULIA ROBERTS

31

Experiencing life as a bumper sticker?

See how you relate to any of the following vehicular vexations:

I have an attitude, and I know how to use it.

I HATE EVERYBODY AND YOU'RE NEXT

ALL STRESSED OUT AND NO ONE TO CHOKE

IT'S BEEN LOVELY, BUT I HAVE TO SCREAM NOW.

If you're living a bumper sticker life, it's time to separate yourself from the self-adhesive sarcasm. There's a whole world out there that would like to know the real you underneath your buzz-kill personality. Don't be one of those bad things that happen to good people.

If someone listens,

or stretches out a hand,

or whispers a kind word

of encouragement,

or attempts to understand

a lonely person,

extraordinary things

begin to happen.

—LORETTA GIRZARTIS

INFINITE RICHES

are all around you if you will open your mental eyes and behold the treasure house of infinity within you. There is a gold mine within you from which you can extract everything you need to live life gloriously, joyously, and abundantly.

—JOSEPH MURPHY

In the confrontation between the stream and the rock the stream always wins—

not through strength,

but through perseverance.

—H. JACKSON BROWN

The heart is happiest when it beats for others.

ABUNDANCE

Most people are deeply scripted in what I call the Scarcity Mentality. They see life as having only so much, as though there were only one pie out there. That's why a character trait that is essential to Win-Win is the Abundance Mentality...that there is plenty out there for everyone.

—STEPHEN R. COVEY, *The 7 Habits of Highly Effective People*

Expect nothing; live frugally on surprise.

—ALICE WALKER

Financial serenity starts when we accept as our truth that money is a state of mind and that abundance is a state of belief. When we choose abundance, we become rich in the real. We attain true wealth. Of course, money is part of personal wealth, but so is **love,** inner peace, harmony, **beauty,** joy, perfect health, **authentic expression,** discovering your bliss, **pursuing your passions, fulfilling your divine destiny.**

—SARAH BAN BREATHNACH

Don't neglect the gifts inside of you.

How to Get into an
ABUNDANCE MENTALITY

1. Start giving regularly. And this doesn't mean giving your opinion or a piece of your mind. It doesn't have to be much—give what you can.

2. Do something generous for others without expecting them to drop to their knees and kiss your feet profusely.

3. Appreciate and feel the richness of life. Learn to be in awe of the little things. Being stoked about big things is fun, but there's nothing wrong with starting small and moving up.

4. Quit saying those three little words: "I can't afford." Stop pleading poverty and acting like a don't-have-won't-have. Attitude is everything. Appreciate what you have first before you ask for more.

5. Write a list of those things that you would like to be more abundant in your life. Then go out and make it happen.

41

In order to

love

how you

live

you must know what

you truly love.

WE TRULY NEED TO
FEEL ABUNDANT

When we are paying attention, a single breath can fill us to overflowing. The touch of a loved one or a moment of sunlight can bring delight to our hearts. The simple gesture of someone's hand resting in our own, a single word of kindness, or a small gift of appreciation can be all we need to feel a tremendous sense of care and well-being. We need so little to feel loved; all we need to do is begin to notice the multitude of tiny gifts and small miracles that punctuate each day we are alive.

—WAYNE MULLER

If at first you

DO

SUCCEED

try not to look astonished!

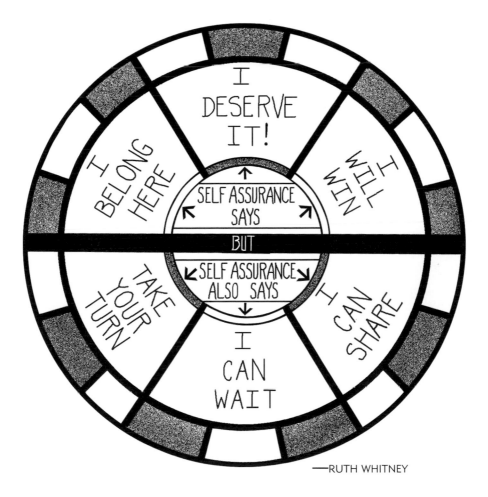

I DESERVE IT!

I BELONG HERE

I WILL WIN

SELF ASSURANCE SAYS

BUT

SELF ASSURANCE ALSO SAYS

TAKE YOUR TURN

I CAN SHARE

I CAN WAIT

—RUTH WHITNEY

45

We have stopped for a moment to encounter each other, to meet, to love, to share. This is a precious moment, but it is transient. It is a little parenthesis in eternity. If we share with caring, lightheartedness, and love, we will create abundance and joy for each other. And then this moment will have been worthwhile.

—DEEPAK CHOPRA

CONNECTION

Without involvement, there is no commitment. Mark it down, asterisk it, circle it, underline it.

———STEPHEN R. COVEY, *The 7 Habits of Highly Effective People*

Things are temporary,
relationships last forever.

Nothing can replace the time we spend

investing in the life of another.

—ROY LESSIN

I'm very loyal in a relationship. Any relationship. When I go out with my mom, I don't look at other moms. I don't go, "Oooooh, I wonder what her macaroni and cheese tastes like."

—GARY SHANDLING

We are **not** here to see through one another. We are here to see one another through.

—CAROL MATTHAU

Once an earthworm popped his head out of the soil and saw a gorgeous earthworm just a few inches from him. Overtaken by the other worm's beauty, he told her, **"I love you... Will you marry me?"** The other worm smiled and answered, "Don't be silly; how can I marry you? I'm your other half!"

—UNKNOWN

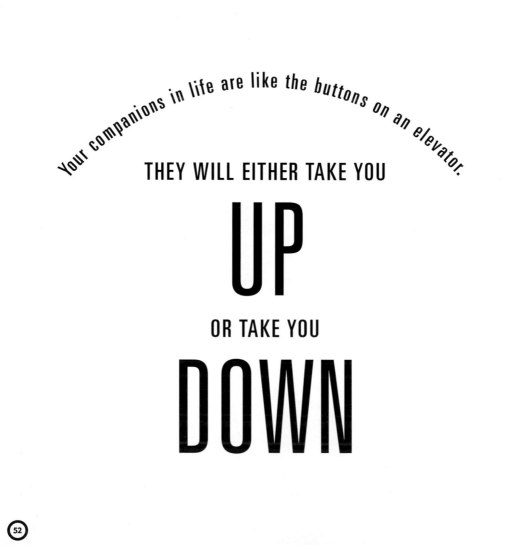

Your companions in life are like the buttons on an elevator.

THEY WILL EITHER TAKE YOU

UP

OR TAKE YOU

DOWN

Find those persons in whose presence you feel more energetic, more creative and more able to pursue your life goals. Stay away from persons who make you feel apprehensive, or who influence you to doubt yourself. Especially, stay away from those persons who drain you, so that your energy is all used up trying to maintain the relationship.

—DENNIS F. AUGUSTINE

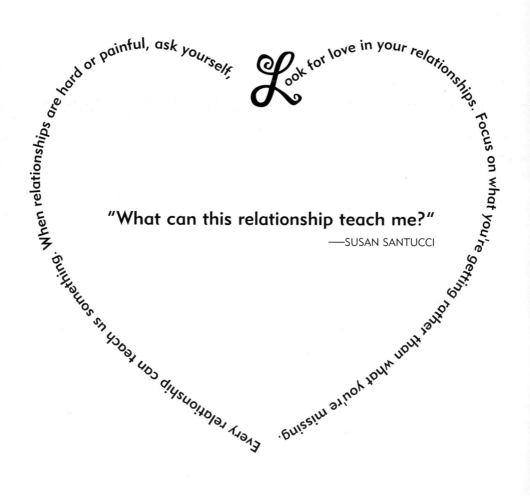

*L*ook for love in your relationships. Focus on what you're getting rather than what you're missing. Every relationship can teach us something. When relationships are hard or painful, ask yourself,

"What can this relationship teach me?"

—SUSAN SANTUCCI

A GOOD FRIEND

is a connection to life,
a tie to the past,
a road to the future,
the key to sanity
in a totally insane world.

—LOIS WYSE

If you look to others for fulfillment,

You will never truly be fulfilled.

If your happiness depends on money,

You will never be happy with yourself.

Be content with what you have;

Rejoice in the way things are.

When you realize there is nothing lacking,

The whole world belongs to you.

—LAO TZU

Some days you're the dog,

some days you're

the hydrant.

"Who's winning in your marriage?" is a ridiculous question.

If both people aren't winning, both are losing.

—STEPHEN R. COVEY

ACCOUNTABILITY

Many people think if you're nice, you're not tough. But Win-Win is nice...and tough. To go for Win-Win, you not only have to be nice, you have to be courageous. You not only have to be empathic, you have to be confident. You not only have to be considerate and sensitive, you have to be brave. To do that, to achieve that balance between courage and consideration, is the essence of real maturity and is fundamental to Win-Win.

—STEPHEN R. COVEY, *The 7 Habits of Highly Effective People*

You have not lived a perfect day, even though you have earned your money, unless you have done something for someone who will never be able to repay you.

—RUTH SMELTZER

The one hand trying to wash itself is a pitiful spectacle, but when one hand washes the other, power is increased, and it becomes a force to be reckoned with.

—MAYA ANGELOU

I had found a kind of serenity, a new maturity…I didn't feel better or

stronger than anyone else but it seemed no longer important whether

everyone loved me or not—more important now was for me to love

them. Feeling that way turns your whole life around; living becomes

the act of giving.

Are you living a bumper sticker life?

Can you relate?

You! Off my planet!

MACHO LAW
prohibits me from admitting I'm wrong

CHAOS, PANIC, & DISORDER.
MY WORK HERE IS DONE.

AND YOUR POINT IS...

The point is your happy button is on perma-hold. Try to see problems as opportunities for a change. The sky is not falling and Chicken Little crossed the road a long time ago. Go ahead and laugh once in a while.

Have faith in yourself.

But have faith in your friends and neighbors, too. I know life is competitive—but it isn't a jungle. Like begets like. Faith inspires faith. People give back substantially what we give them.

—UNKNOWN

*G*ratitude unlocks the fullness of life. It turns what we have into enough, and more. It turns denial into acceptance, chaos to order, confusion to clarity. It can turn a meal into a feast, a house into a home, a stranger into a friend. Gratitude makes sense of our past, brings peace for today, and creates a vision for tomorrow.

—MELODY BEATTIE

It might LOOK like I'm doing nothing,

but at the cellular level I'm really quite busy.

True power is knowing that you can, but you don't.

—JULIET ALICIA JARVIS

Everyone has a photographic memory. Some don't have film.

COOPERATION

With a Win-Win solution, all parties feel good about the decision and feel committed to the action plan. Win-Win sees life as a cooperative, not a competitive arena.

——STEPHEN R. COVEY, *The 7 Habits of Highly Effective People*

If we don't help each other, who will help us?

We are here
on earth to
do good
to others.

What the others are here for, I don't know.

—W. H. AUDEN

Her little girl was late arriving home from school so the mother began to scold her daughter, but stopped and asked, "Why are you so late?"

"I had to help another girl. She was in trouble," replied the daughter.

"What did you do to help her?"

"Oh, I sat down and helped her cry."

—UNKNOWN

We are each of us angels with only one wing, and **we can only fly by embracing one another.**

—LUCIANO DE CRESCENZO

If someone can stand on my shoulders and take their dream to a higher level, maybe that's success, too.

—STEVE POTTER

Life

is a series of delicate meetings

held together by a spider's thread

strong as a steel span, tender

as the wind blowing it all away.

—SANDRA BERNHARD

MR. SPOCK: May I point out that I had an opportunity to observe your counterparts quite closely. They were brutal, savage, unprincipled, uncivilized, and treacherous——in every way, splendid examples of homo sapiens. The very flower of humanity. I found them quite refreshing.

CAPTAIN KIRK: I'm not sure, but I think we've been insulted.

—*STAR TREK*

We are visitors on this planet. We are here for ninety, one hundred years at the very most. During that period, we must try to do something good, something useful with our lives. Try to be at peace with yourself, and help others share that peace. If you contribute to other people's happiness, you will find the goal, the true meaning of life.

—DALAI LAMA

I discovered a long time ago that if I helped people get what they wanted,

I would always get what I wanted and I would never have to worry.

—ANTHONY ROBBINS

Bumper sticker life? Part III

You know the drill:

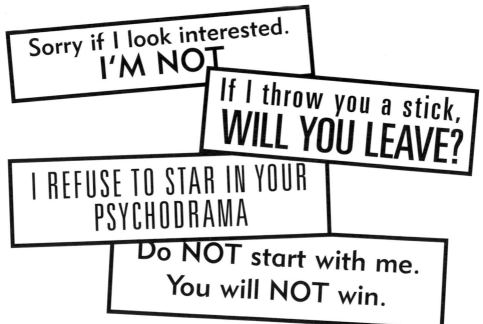

Sorry if I look interested.
I'M NOT

If I throw you a stick,
WILL YOU LEAVE?

I REFUSE TO STAR IN YOUR
PSYCHODRAMA

Do NOT start with me.
You will NOT win.

If you relate to the preceding bumper stickers, your bandwidth is shrinking at a rapid rate. Realize that the life you desire has more to do with what you get rid of than what you keep. As in your attitude. Therapy is expensive, poppin' bubble wrap is cheap. You decide.

Co-Dependents' Support Group:

"Let's help each other to stop helping each other!"

—LAURA ARDIEL

PERFORMANCE

I am always amazed at the results that happen, both to individuals and to organizations, when responsible, proactive, self-directing individuals are turned loose on a task.

—STEPHEN R. COVEY, *The 7 Habits of Highly Effective People*

Be so good they can't ignore you.

—JERRY DUNN

EXPERIENCE

is what you get when you don't get what you want.

—UNKNOWN

LIFE IS A JOURNEY,

and if you open yourself up to its possibilities, it can take you in directions you never imagined. A rich life doesn't necessarily take you there wrapped in cashmere, weighted with gold, or traveling first-class. You need not compete with anyone else. Your journey is your own.

—SUZE ORMAN

It's hard to make a comeback

when you haven't been anywhere.

Life is a smorgasbord for bellyachers, an endless buffet of tightwad bosses, lost earrings, exploding pens. There's always something to be depressed about. But that's so…depressing. Snap out of it! Being swell isn't just about smooth movers… it's about having the right spirit. Chin up, as they used to say. We call it pathological optimism. Either way sounds corny. But it's the

Soul of Swell:

knowing how to make the bad times good and the good times unforgettable.

—CYNTHIA ROWLEY AND ILENE ROSENZWEIG

PEOPLE CAN BE DIVIDED INTO 3 GROUPS:

Those who **make** things happen.

Those who **watch** things happen.

Those who **wonder** what happened.

—UNKNOWN

When you're finally holding all the cards, why does everyone else decide to play chess?

*F*ear of success is one of the new fears I've heard about. And I think it's definitely a sign we're running out of fears. A person suffering from fear of success is scraping the bottom of the barrel. Are we going to need AA-type meetings for these people? They get up to the microphone and go, "Hi, my name is Bill and I can't stand the thought of having a stereo and a cream colored couch?"

—JERRY SEINFELD

If you want

a place in the sun,

you have to expect some blisters.

—UNKNOWN

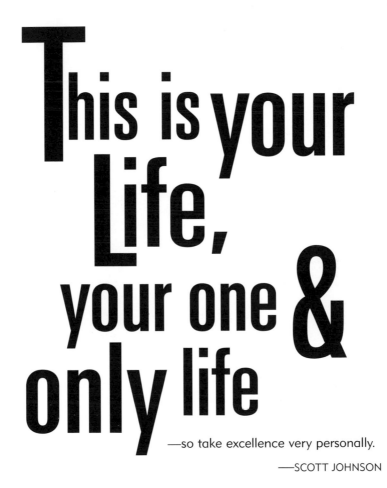

This is your Life, your one & only life

—so take excellence very personally.

—SCOTT JOHNSON

We are so conditioned to see life as a competition that in order to declare a winner, we must also declare a loser. And heaven forbid it should end up in a tie.

PERSPECTIVE

If two people have the same opinion, one is not necessary...I don't want to talk, to communicate, with someone who agrees with me; I want to communicate with you because you see it differently. I value that difference.

—STEPHEN R. COVEY, *The 7 Habits of Highly Effective People*

We must not, in trying to

think about how we can make

a big difference, ignore the small

daily differences we can make

which, over time, add up to

big differences that we often

cannot foresee.

—MARION WRIGHT EDELMAN

Do you worry LESS about what other people think about you and MORE about what you think of them?

The Chinese word for

CRISIS

consists of two characters:

one represents
"danger"
and the other
"hidden opportunity."

—M. SCOTT PECK

Can I trade this life for
what's behind Door Number 2?

97

Compassion

is the ability to totally imagine what it is like
to be an other, the force that makes a bridge from
the island of one individual to the island of the other.
It is an ability to step outside our own perspective,
limitations and ego, and become attentive in a
vulnerable, encouraging, critical, and creative way
with the hidden world of another person.

—JOHN O'DONOHUE

We who lived in concentration camps can remember the men who walked through the huts comforting others, giving away their last piece of bread. They may have been few in number, but they offer sufficient proof that **everything can be taken from a man but one thing:** the last of the human freedoms—to choose one's attitude in any given set of circumstances.

—VIKTOR FRANKL

Judgments
prevent us from seeing the good that lies beyond appearances.

—WAYNE DYER

DO YOU NEED
A NICENESS SUPPORT GROUP?

There is such a thing as being "too nice" if it costs you your integrity. There's no need to put up with everything that comes your way with a big cheery smile and footprints on your back. Take this quiz to see if you suffer from chronic niceness.

———

Do you have a problem confronting others even if you know what they've done is wrong?

———

Do you find yourself saying "yes" when you'd rather say "don't even go there"?

———

Do you walk away from disagreements so many times that you've memorized the pattern of the floor tile?

———

Have you ever told a friend an absolute lie rather than hurt his or her feelings?

———

Do you apologize for everything from having an opinion to taking the last available table at the local coffeehouse?

———

If you answered "yes" to any of the above questions, consider giving your "niceness" a day off. There's nothing wrong with asserting yourself. Just do it in a Win-Win manner and you'll end up making everyone happy. Most of all, yourself.

I didn't lose the gold.
I WON the silver.

—MICHELLE KWAN

Success comes in

CANS.

Failure comes in

CAN'TS.

I have missed more than 9,000 shots in my career. I have lost almost 300 games. On 26 occasions I have been entrusted to take the game-winning shot…and missed. I have failed over and over again in my life. And that is why I succeed.

——MICHAEL JORDAN

ACHIEVEMENT

The stronger you are—the more genuine your character, the higher your level of proactivity, the more committed you really are to Win-Win—the more powerful your influence will be with another person. This is the real test of interpersonal relationships.

——STEPHEN R. COVEY, *The 7 Habits of Highly Effective People*

Happiness is not having what you want—but wanting what you have.

Getting your financial house in order means valuing people over money, and valuing money over things. It means putting money in the right place in your heart, and in the right investments. It means having all that you love, and loving all that you have. It means turning toward your money, and turning your money, some of your money, toward righteous causes. But **money alone**, as important as it is, **can never make you truly rich.**

—SUZE ORMAN

TRUST YOURSELF.

Create the kind of self that you will be happy to live with all your life. Make the most of yourself by fanning the tiny, inner sparks of possibility into flames of achievement.

—FOSTER C. McCLELLAN

I want to put a ding in the universe.

—STEVE JOBS

It's true that we don't know what we've got until we lose it,

but it's also true that **we don't know what we've been missing until it arrives.**

—UNKNOWN

Authentic success

is knowing that if you left the world today,

you'd leave with no regrets.

No one lives long enough to learn everything they need to learn starting from scratch. To be successful, we absolutely, positively have to find people who have already paid the price to learn the things that we need to learn to achieve our goals.

—BRIAN TRACY

Why does success always happen in private

and failure in full view?

The adventure is over. Everything gets over...

except the part you carry with you.

—E. L. KONIGSBURG

Is that your FINAL answer?

About Franklin Covey

Franklin Covey is the world's leading time management and life leadership company. Based on proven principles, our services and products are used by more than 15 million people worldwide. We work with a wide variety of clients, Fortune 500 material, as well as smaller companies, communities, and organizations. You may know us from our world-renowned Franklin Planner or any of our books in the 7 Habits series. By the way, Franklin Covey books have sold over 15 million copies worldwide—over 1½ million each year. But what you may not know about Franklin Covey is we also offer leadership training, motivational workshops, personal coaching, audiotapes and videotapes, and *PRIORITIES* magazine just to name a few.

Let Us Know What You Think

We'd love to hear your suggestions or comments about *Abundance: Fulfilling Your Potential for Success* or any of our Portable 7 Habits books.

www.franklincovey.com/portable7

The Portable 7 Habits
Franklin Covey
MS0733-CK
2200 West Parkway Boulevard
Salt Lake City, Utah 84119-2331 USA

1-800-952-6839
International (801) 229-1333 Fax (801) 229-1233

RECOMMENDED READING

Boldt, Laurence G. *The Tao of Abundance: Eight Ancient Principles for Abundant Living*. Viking Penguin, 1999.

Breathnach, Sarah Ban. *Something More: Excavating Your Authentic Self*. Warner Books, 1998.

——. *The Simple Abundance Companion*. Warner Books, 2000.

Don't Worry Make Money: Spiritual and Practical Ways to Create Abundance and More Fun in Your Life. Hyperion, 1997.

Carter-Scott, Chérie. *If Love Is a Game, These Are the Rules*. Broadway Books, 1999.

Chodron, Pema. *When Things Fall Apart: Heart Advice for Difficult Times*. Shambala, 1997.

Covey, Stephen R. *The 7 Habits of Highly Effective People*. Simon & Schuster, 1989.

——. *Living the 7 Habits*. Simon & Schuster, 1999.

Dershowitz, Barbara. *Affluent Spirit: Lessons in Spiritual and Material Abundance*. BDC, 1995.

Dwyer, Wayne W. *Manifest Your Destiny*. Whitaker House, 1997.

Gattuso, Joan. *A Course in Life*. Jeremy P. Tarcher/Putnam, 1998.

Gray, John. *Mars and Venus Starting Over*. HarperCollins,1998.

——. *Men Are from Mars, Women Are from Venus*. HarperTrade, 1992.

Hobday, Jose. *Stories of Awe and Abundance*. Continuum International, 1999.

Kudlow, Lawrence A. *American Abundance: The New Economics and Moral Prosperity*. American Heritage, 1998.

Larned, Marianne. *Stone Soup for the World: Life-Changing Stories of Kindness*

& *Courageous Acts of Service*. Fine Communications, 1999.

Orman, Suze. *The Courage to Be Rich: Creating a Life of Material and Spiritual Abundance*. Riverhead Books, 1999.

Prager, Marcia. *The Path to Blessing: Experiencing the Energy and Abundance of the Divine*. Crown Publishing Group, 1999.

Ramsey, Dave. *Financial Peace*. Viking, 1992, 1995.

———. *How to Have More Than Enough: A Step-by-Step Guide to Creating Abundance*. Penguin USA, 2000.

Roman, Sanaya, and Duane Packer. *Keys to Abundance, Vol. 1*. Starseed Press, 1988.

Santucci, Susan. *Pathways to the Spirit*. Hyperion, 1999.

Sutherland, Paul H. *Zenvesting: The Art of Abundance and Managing Money*. Ten Speed, 1999.

VanZant, Iyanla. *Faith in the Valley*. Simon & Schuster, 1998.

Waldman, Jackie, and Janis Leibs Dworkis. *The Courage to Give: Inspiring Stories of People Who Triumphed over Tragedy and Made a Difference in the World*. Conari Press, 1999.

Walsch, Neale Donald. *Abundance and Right Livlihood: Applications for Living*. Hampton Roads, 1999.

Williamson, Marianne. *A Return to Love*. HarperPerennial, 1992.

———. *Abundance* (4 cassettes). Hay House Inc., 1999.